To Kristen

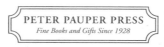

PETER PAUPER PRESS
Fine Books and Gifts Since 1928

OUR COMPANY

In 1928, at the age of twenty-two, Peter Beilenson began printing books on a small press in the basement of his parents' home in Larchmont, New York. Peter—and later, his wife, Edna—sought to create fine books that sold at "prices even a pauper could afford."

Today, still family owned and operated, Peter Pauper Press continues to honor our founders' legacy—and our customers' expectations—of beauty, quality, and value.

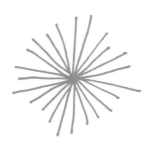

Published by Peter Pauper Press, Inc.
202 Mamaroneck Avenue
White Plains, New York 10601
All rights reserved
ISBN 978-1-4413-1748-3
Printed in China
7   6   5   4
Visit us at www.peterpauper.com

THE RULES OF THIS BOOK:

There are no rules.

There is no right or wrong way to use this book.

Take your time. Have FUN.

Try crazy stuff.

Trust yourself. Don't judge. Turn off your filters.

Don't just look at these pages. USE them.

There is no right or wrong way to make art.

When the instructions say "draw," you can replace this with "paint" or "scratch" or "smudge" or "carve" or whatever you want.

You don't have to show this book to anyone.
It can be a secret.

It's impossible to screw up. Did I mention that already?

Okay. Let's make some art!

ARE YOU READY?

LET'S GO!

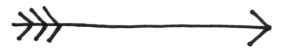

Draw hands on this clock so that it's three hours earlier than now.

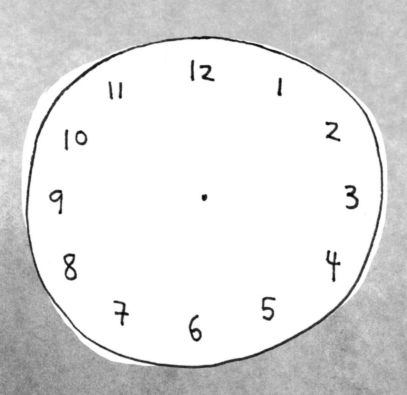

Good. Now you have more time to create.

Draw or paint or write something that makes you feel AMAZING.

My preferred name is

ELLIOT

also, girls are hot

DRAW YOUR BARE FEET.

Toes are weird and fun to draw.

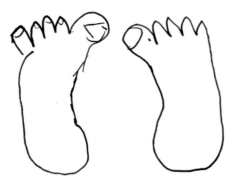

Imagine you used this big magnet to pick up a variety of metal objects. Draw all the things that are now stuck to the magnet.

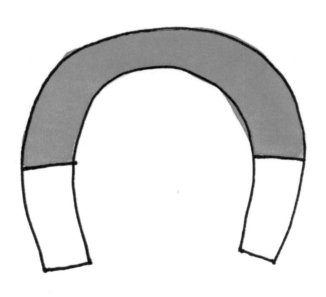

Draw or paint (or describe with words)
your favorite place to be.

Draw an airplane flying by.

Draw the box of your favorite breakfast cereal.

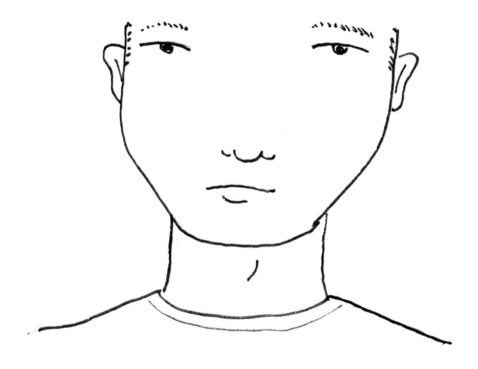

Draw a hat on this gal.

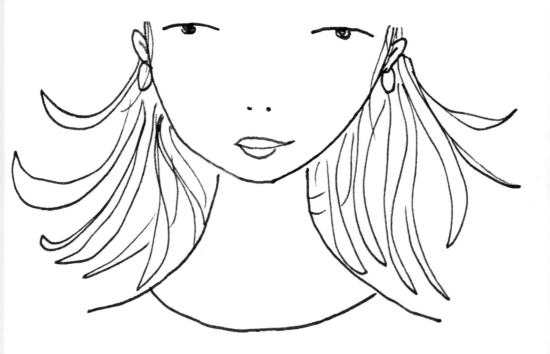

DRAW WITH TRIANGLES

Let's make images using only triangles.
Like this:

a table

the letter 'E'

a face

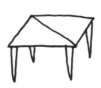

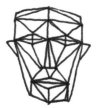

It's pretty simple.
Start with one triangle:

Draw more triangles
attached together:

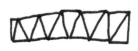

Keep building up your
image until you're done:

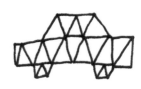

a car

Using only triangles, draw a SUITCASE.

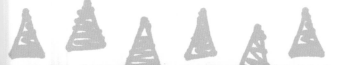

Using only triangles, draw a TABLE.

Draw what's happening inside this car.

Sometimes fancy art supplies
can be intimidating.

Draw something on this roll
of toilet paper.

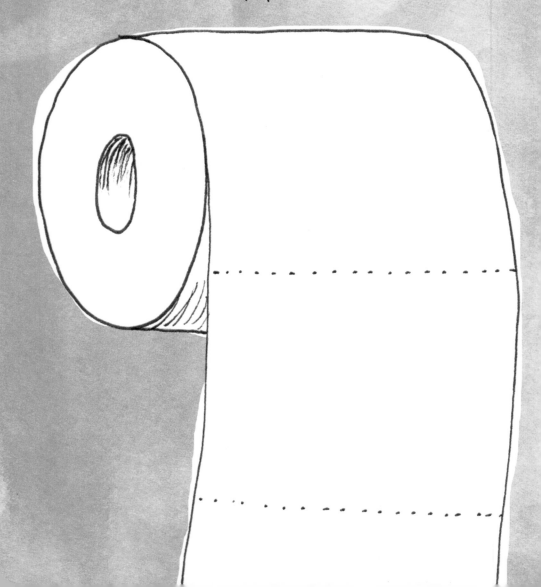

Draw something on this placemat.

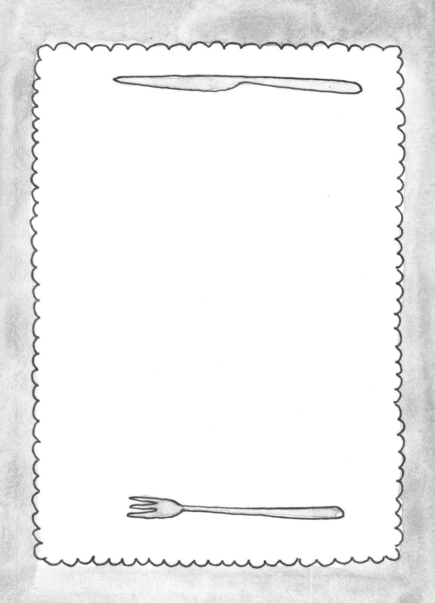

CONNECT THE DOTS

On the following page we are going to connect the dots to create pictures. Use just a few dots, or use a lot.

Here's an example:

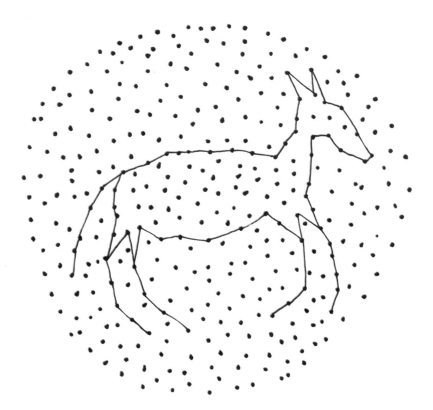

Okay, let's go!

Connect the dots to make a FISH.

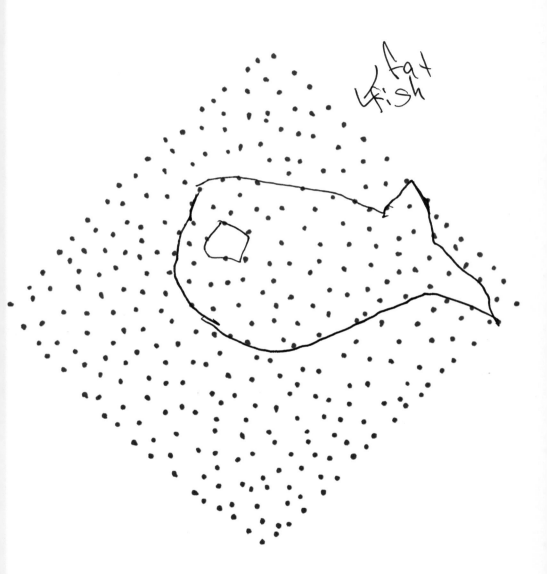

fat
4fish

Draw something inside this
rainbow shape, but DON'T
draw a rainbow:

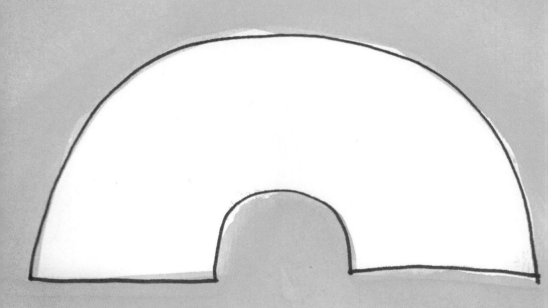

Okay, you can draw a
rainbow in this one.

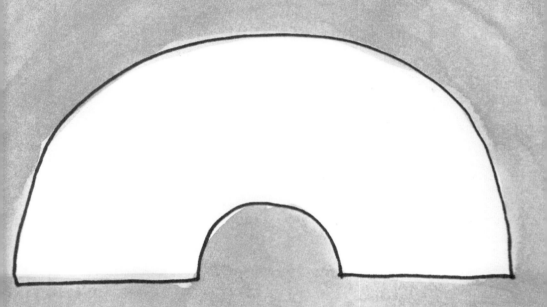

Connect the dots to make a HAT.

happy man
:D

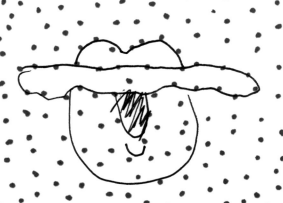

Draw a flower
(from memory, from your garden, from a photo...).

Draw or paint or write something
that makes you feel HOPEFUL.

Using only triangles, draw a TRUMPET.

Draw something that rhymes with NOOK.

Design a tattoo for a serious rock 'n' roll fan.

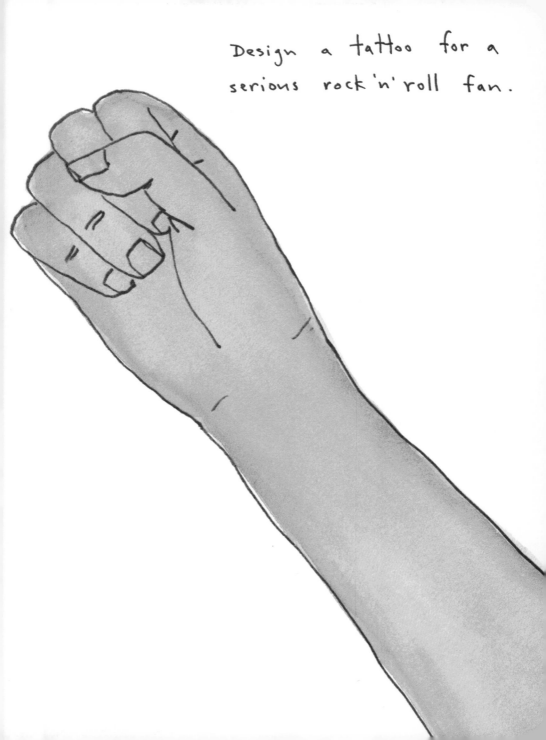

Draw a fantastical flower that doesn't exist (but maybe should).

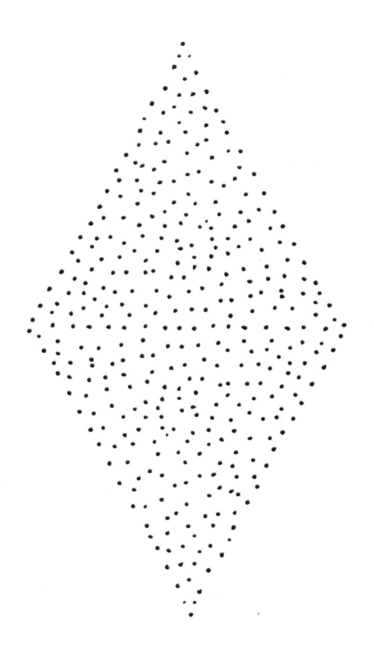

TURN THIS INTO SOMETHING

It's fun to turn nondescript shapes into things we (sort of) recognize.

There are lots of ways to do it, and there are <u>no</u> wrong ways.

Examples:

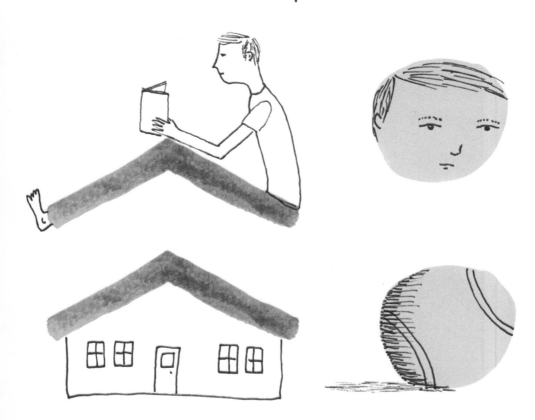

Turn this into something. Anything!

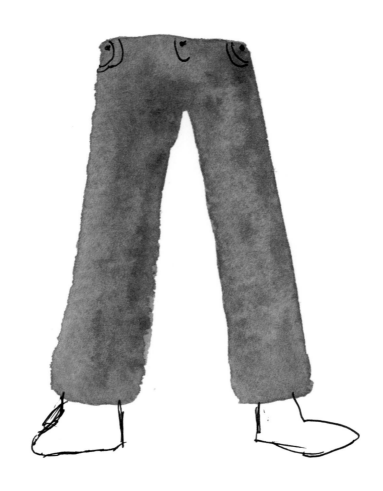

Draw or paint something
that makes you feel CALM.

Draw something that rhymes with MAIL.

Connect the dots to make a PHONE.

Turn this into something.

Turn this into something. Anything!

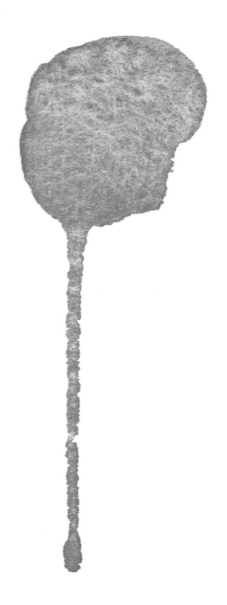

Connect the dots to make a FORK.

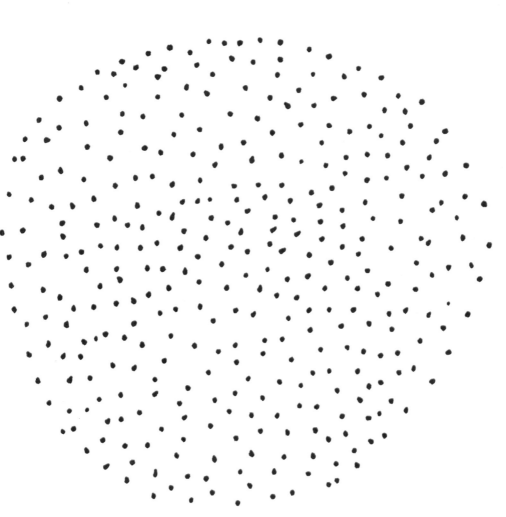

Draw what's in your pockets right now.

I magine you have your own
coffee company. What would you
call it, and what would be your logo?

Draw it on the cup.

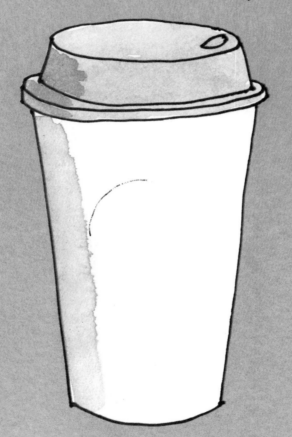

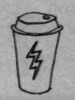

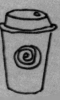

Draw a skull.

(It doesn't matter if it looks bad.
The skull won't care — he's dead.)

Decorate this tote bag with nature (animals or trees or flowers or...).

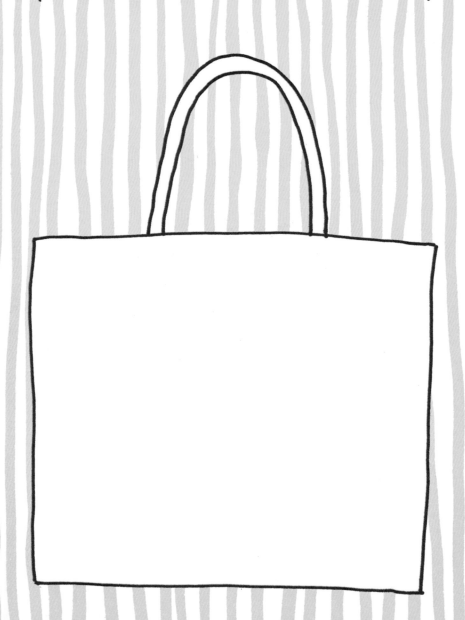

Turn this into something.

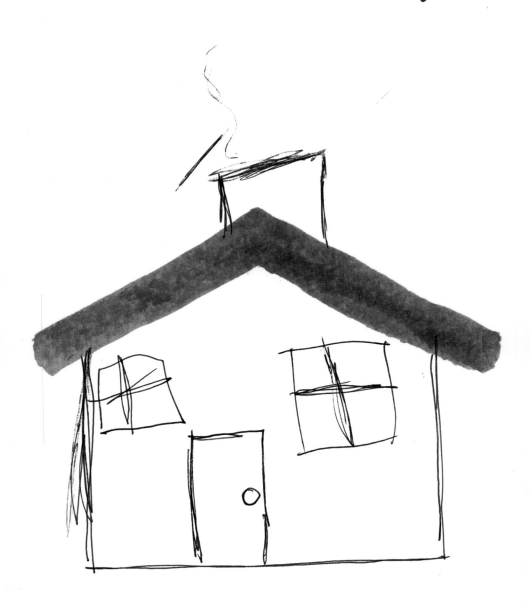

Make a line or a scribble
or an image that expresses
FLOW.

(oooh. I like that.)

Design a tattoo
for someone who
recently lost
a pet bird.

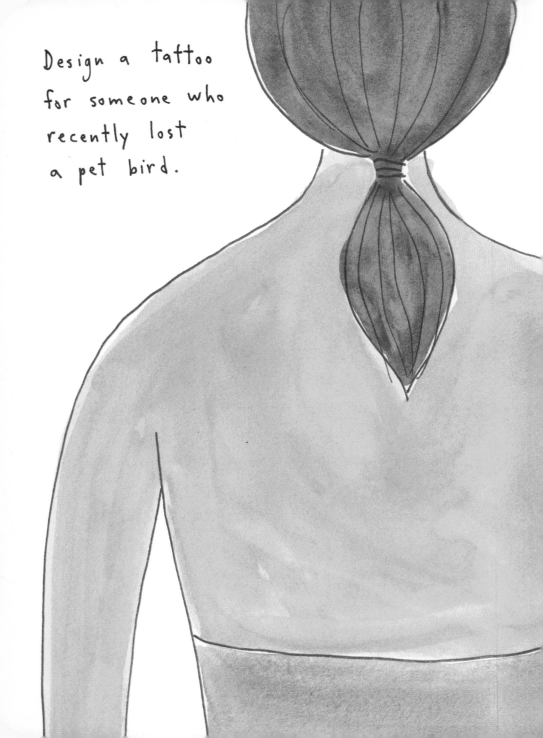

What's your mood right now? Draw it.
(You can use words too.)

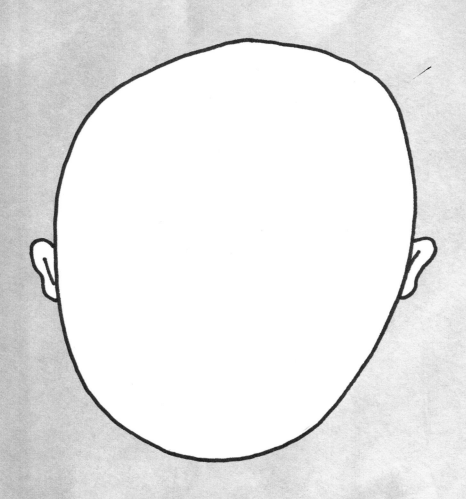

Using only triangles, draw a FACE.

Turn this into something.

Make your own versions of the
king and Queen of Hearts.

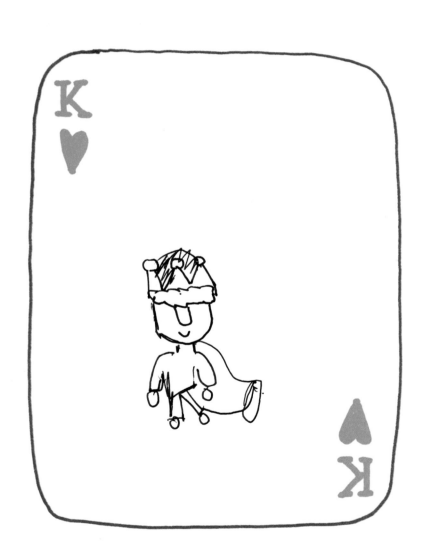

who doesnt love it when the lady is in charge?

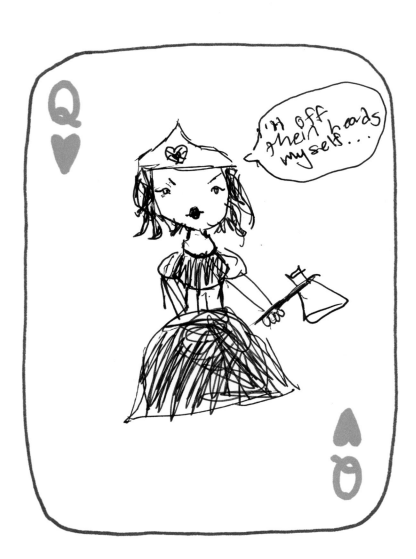

Okay, this time make your own King and Queen of Hearts, but don't draw any people.

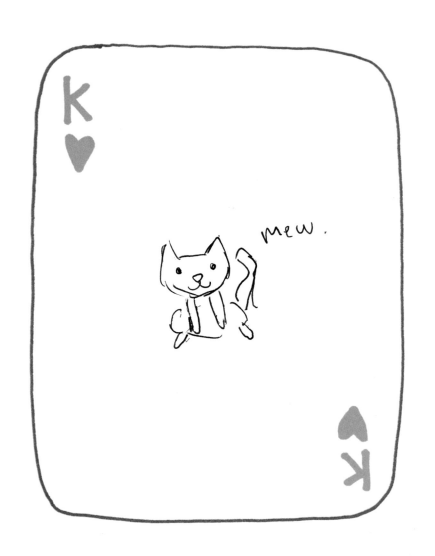

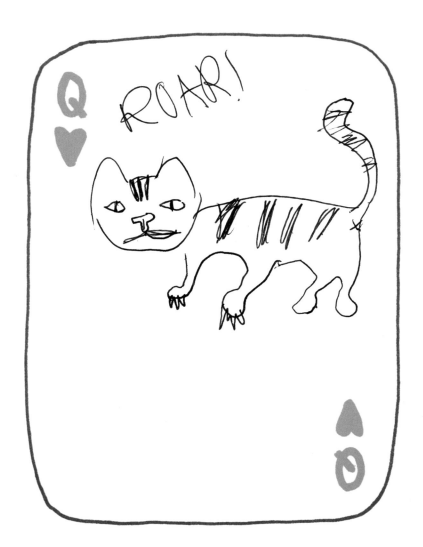

Using only triangles, draw an OWL.

Make a line or a scribble
or an image that expresses
EXCITEMENT.

(Yeah! That's great!)

Draw or paint an object that
makes you feel GOOD.

Make this person look COOL.

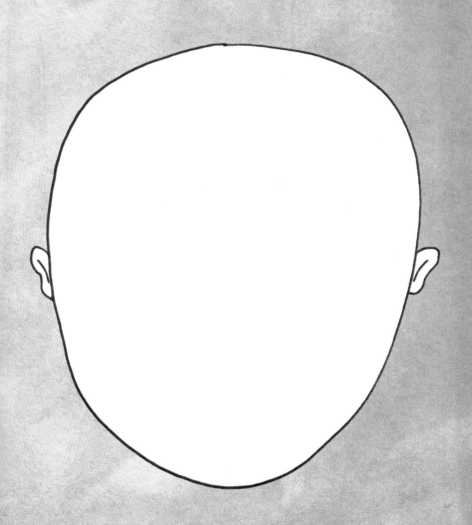

Draw on these rocks.

Draw faces, patterns, words, secrets, mysterious prehistoric symbols, etc.

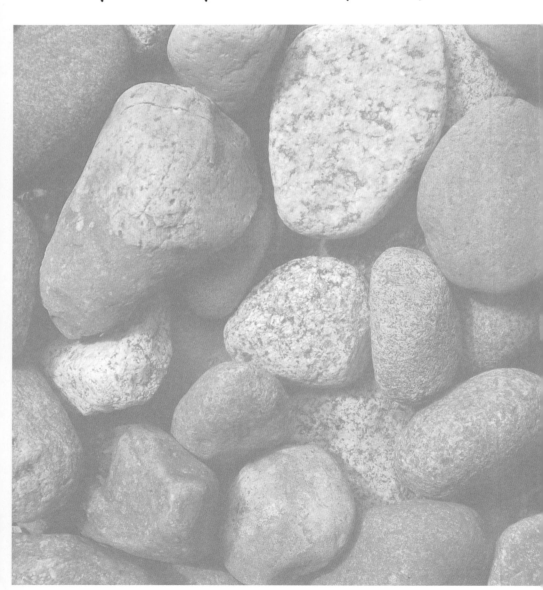

Draw or write or paint something
that makes you feel POWERFUL.

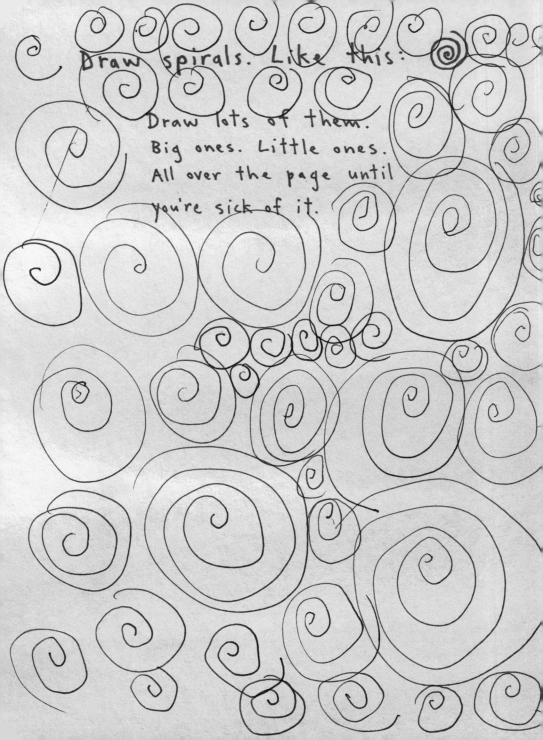

Draw spirals. Like this:

Draw lots of them.
Big ones. Little ones.
All over the page until
you're sick of it.

Okay, now draw a square within a square within a square...

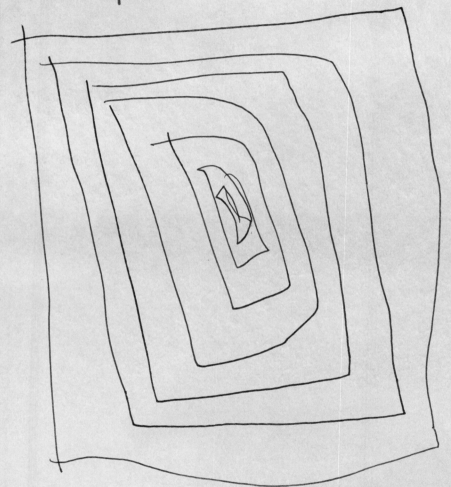

Aaah...
Feels good to draw squares.

Connect the dots to make a BICYCLE.

Draw the art award that you will win one day.

HELPFUL SIGN

Write some good advice or an inspirational quote on this sign.

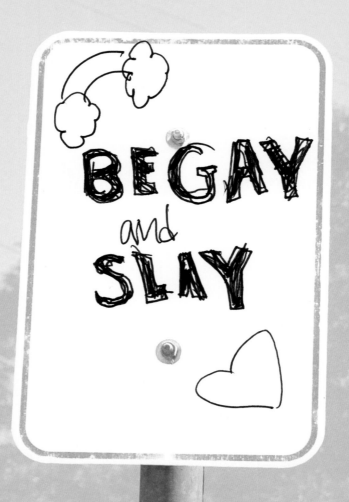

Connect the dots to make a HORSE.

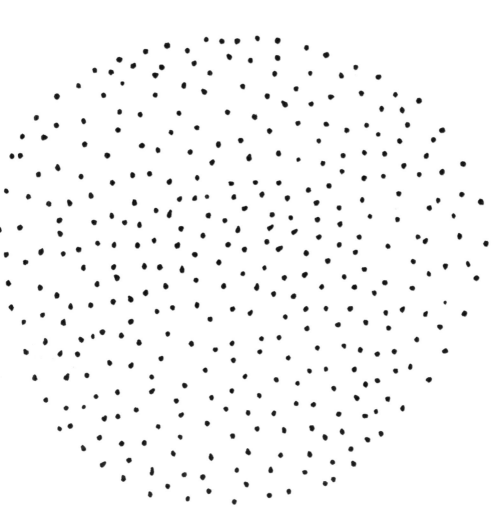

Draw or paint (or write about) something
that gives you COMFORT.

Draw a hand with 6 fingers.

(Imagine how fast you could type if you
had 6 fingers on each hand! Crazy.)

What's your mood going to be tomorrow?
Draw it. (You can use words too if you want.)

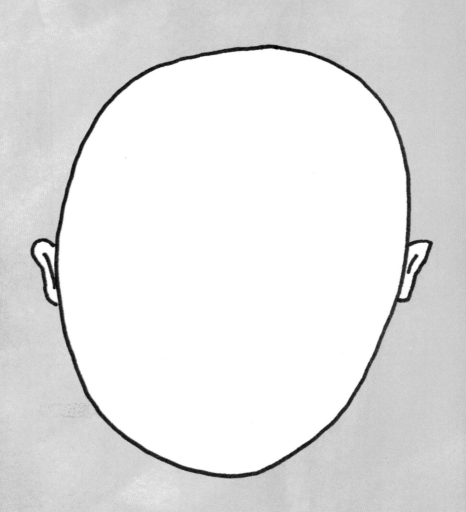

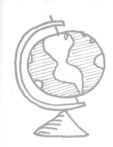

Draw or paint (or write about) a place you'd like to go to.

Decorate this tote bag with words (a favorite expression, a funny or inspirational quote), etc.).

die

Draw something that rhymes with DIRT.

See this?
This is WOOD GRAIN.
(It's so fun to draw!)

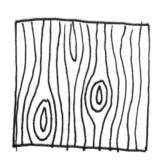

Draw wood grain on these objects.

a log

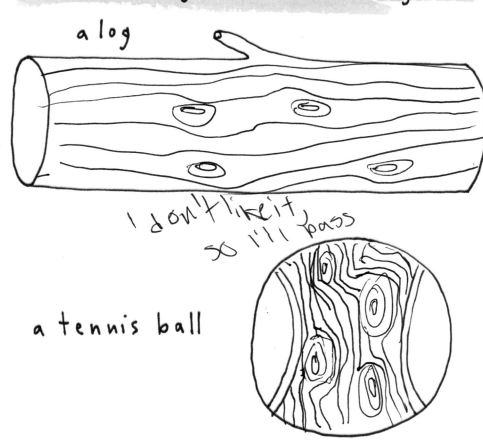

I don't like it
so I'll pass

a tennis ball

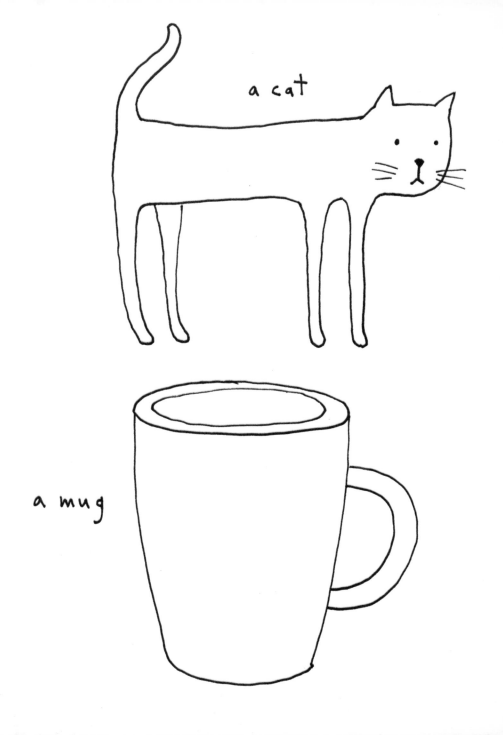

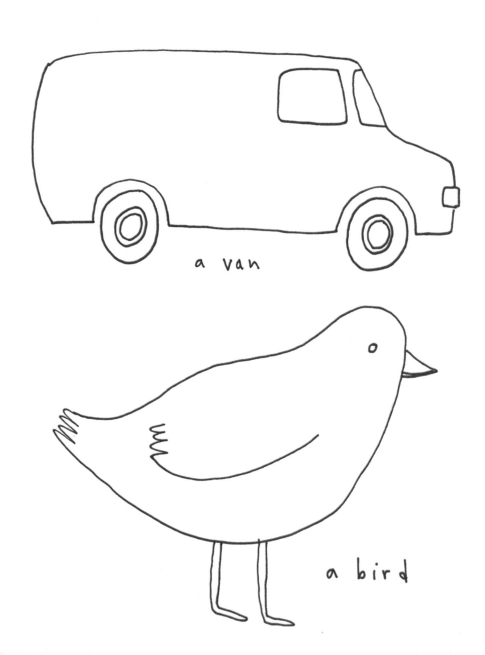

a van

a bird

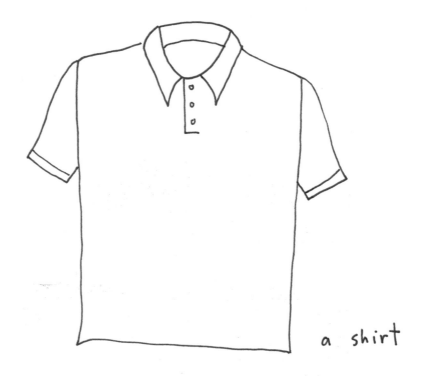

a shirt

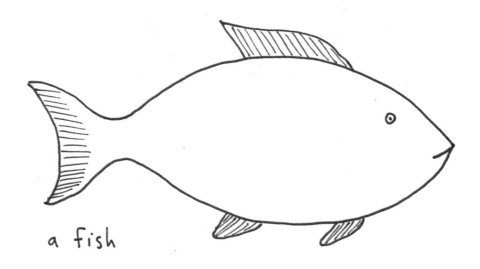

a fish

PIXEL PICTURES

Color in the squares to make a picture.

Here's an example:

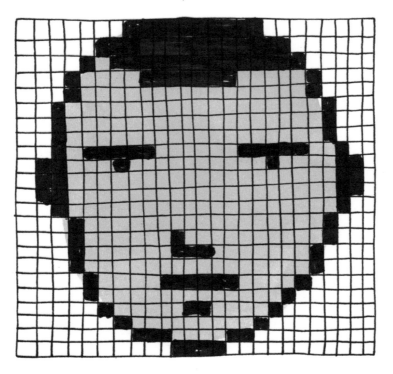

Hint: Draw an outline of your picture
in pencil first, then color in
the squares.

Okay, now it's your turn...

Color in the squares to make a face.

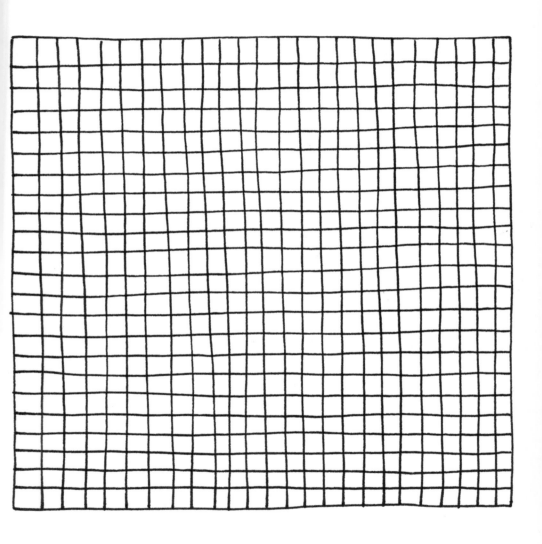

Using only triangles, draw a SHARK.

Make this man look HAPPY.

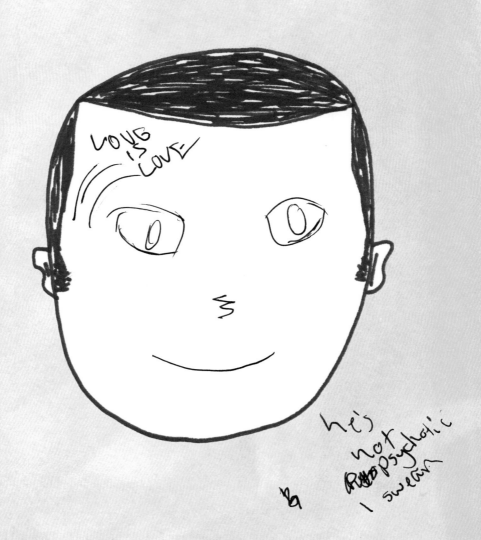

Using only triangles, draw a TRUCK.

Draw a snowman using 10 snowballs
(not the usual 2 or 3).

maybe like this →

or this →

Color in the squares to make a house.

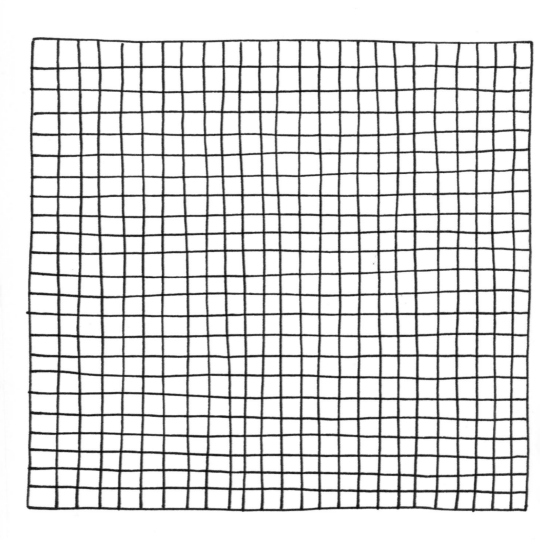

Turn this into something. Anything!

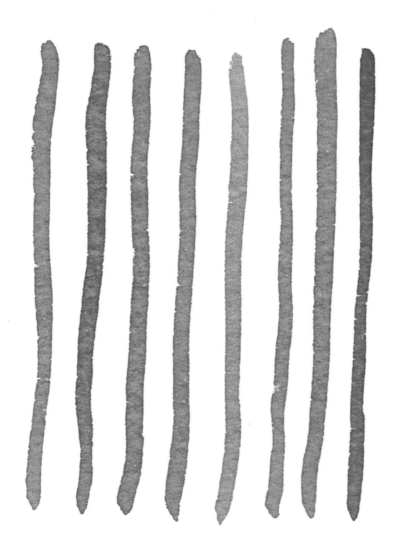

Draw something that rhymes with FAR.

Turn this into something.

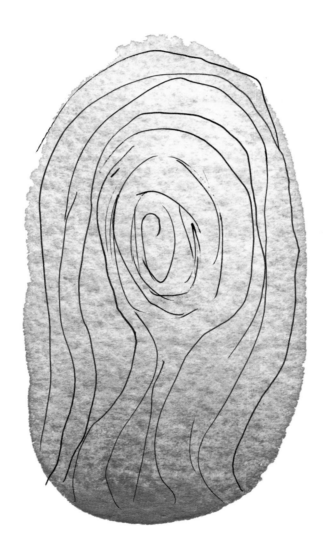

Color in the squares to make a tree.

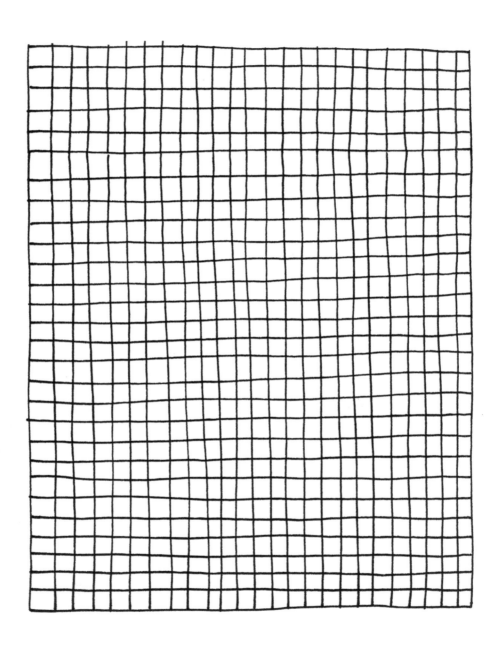

Make this woman look HAPPY.

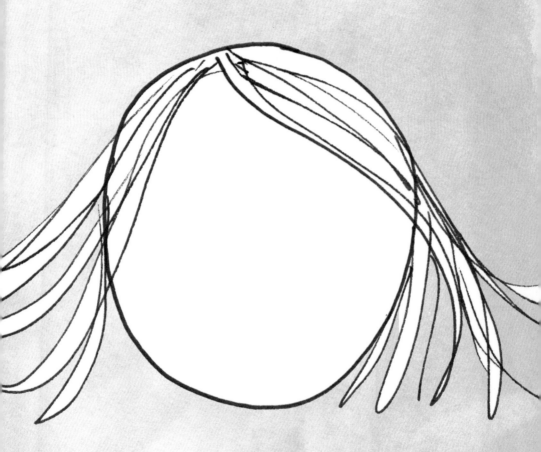

Turn this into something. Anything!

DRAW YOUR SHOES.

Draw them on your feet or off.
Whichever way you want.

Turn this into something.

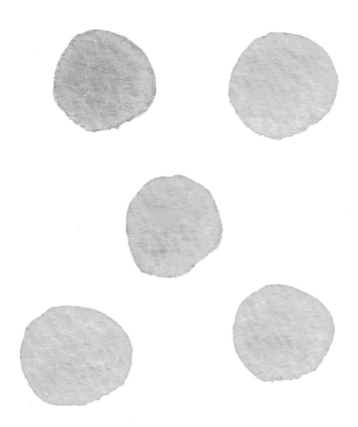

Make this person look like YOU.

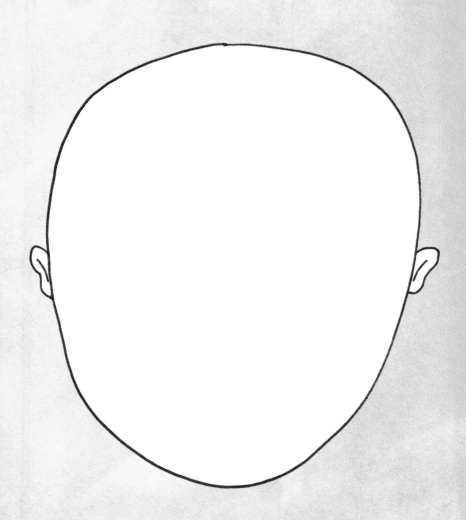

Draw a UFO in the sky.

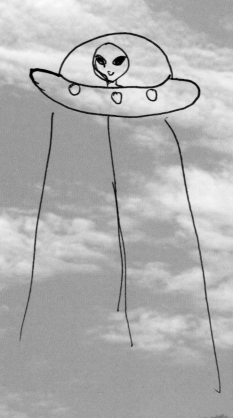

Color in the squares to make a tea cup.

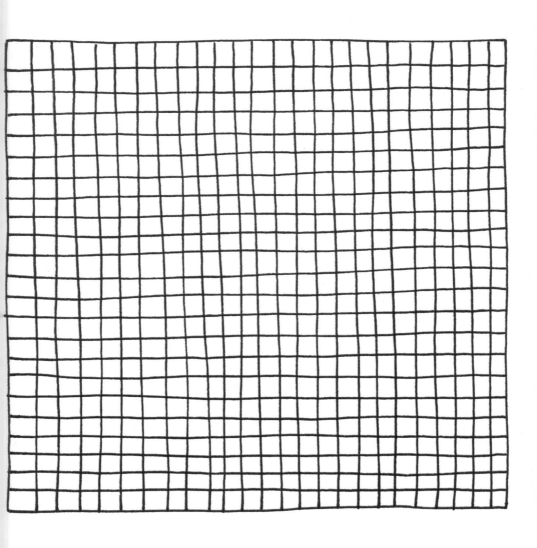

If you're unsure about your ability to do something in this book, this page has the answer.

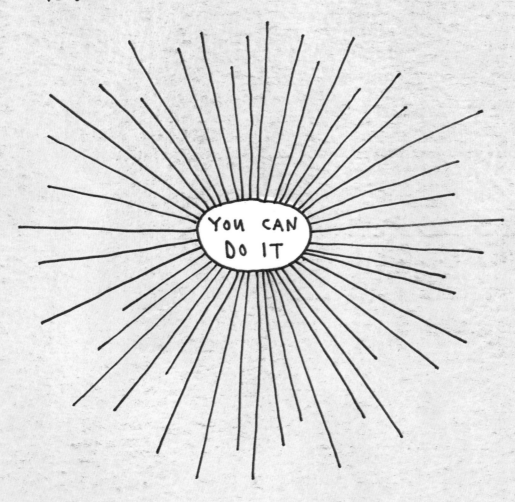

Refer to this page as often as necessary.

Using only triangles, draw a PAIR OF SOCKS.

Draw something that rhymes with BAG.

(If you can't think of anything, just draw a bag!)

Color in the squares to make a bird.

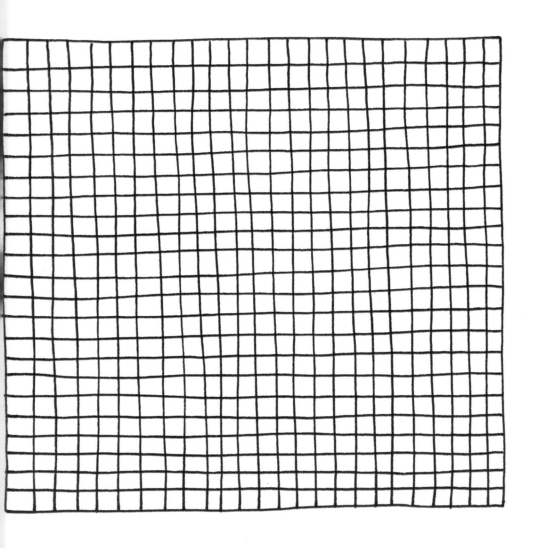

Decorate this mug for someone who enjoys a strong jolt of coffee.

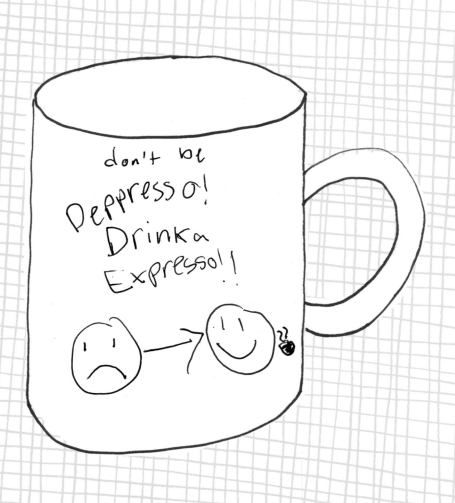

Design a tattoo for someone
who loves to barbeque.

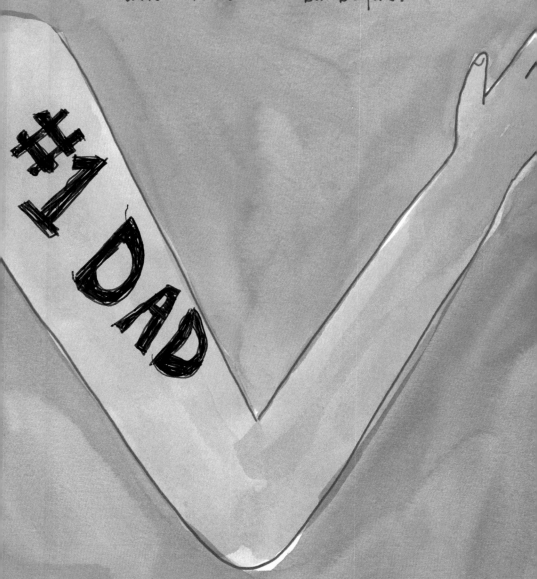

Using only triangles, draw a SUBMARINE.

Draw something that rhymes with SKY.

Design a tattoo for someone who loves the ocean.

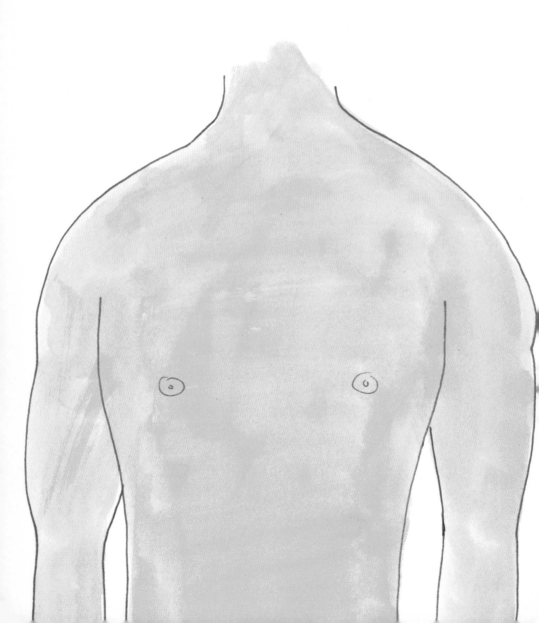

Make this person look CONFUSED.

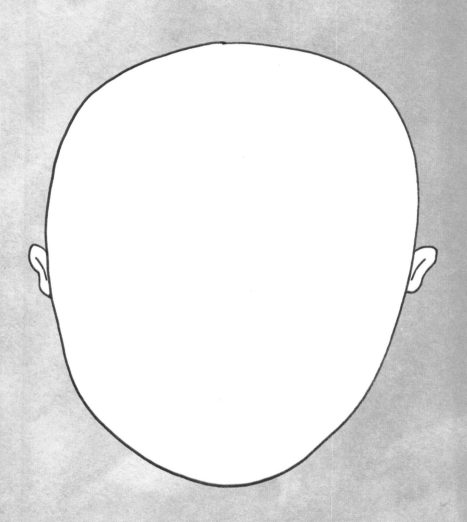

Draw something that rhymes with ORANGE.

Okay, nothing rhymes with orange.
So just draw an orange.

Draw a chair using only two lines.

Draw a face using only three lines.

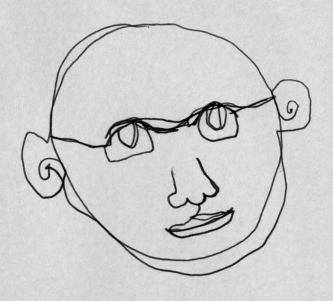

Draw something that rhymes with STONE.

Make this person look SAD.

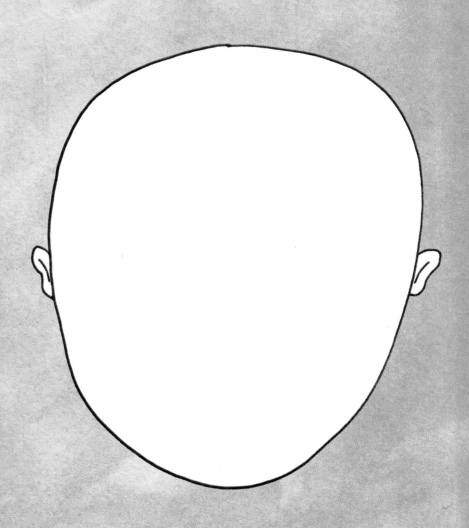

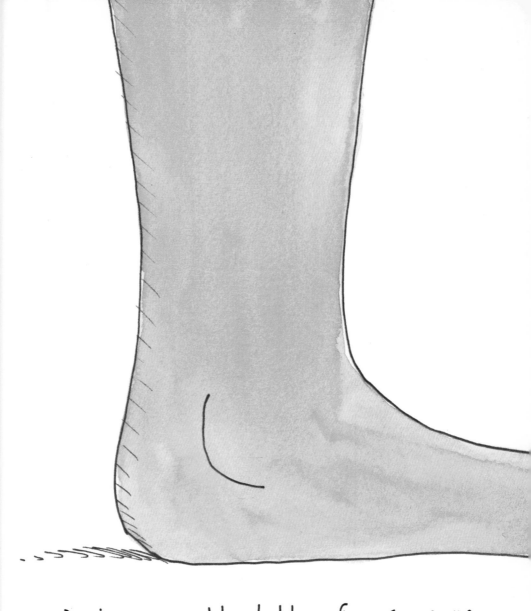

Design an ankle tattoo for someone who thinks minivans are cool.

(who says they aren't?)

Draw something that rhymes with TOFFEE.

write or draw your secret
ambition on this bottle.

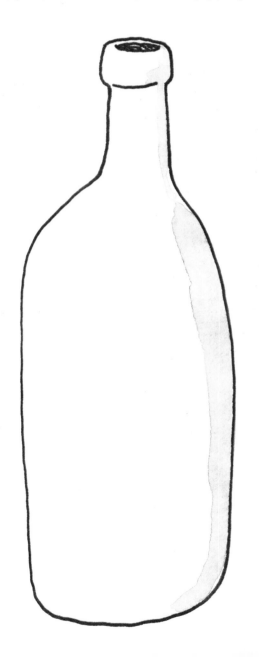

Color in the squares to make a banana.

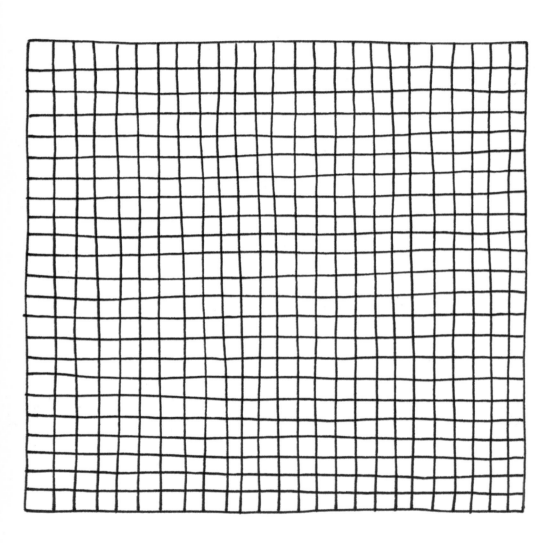

Make this person look YOUNG.

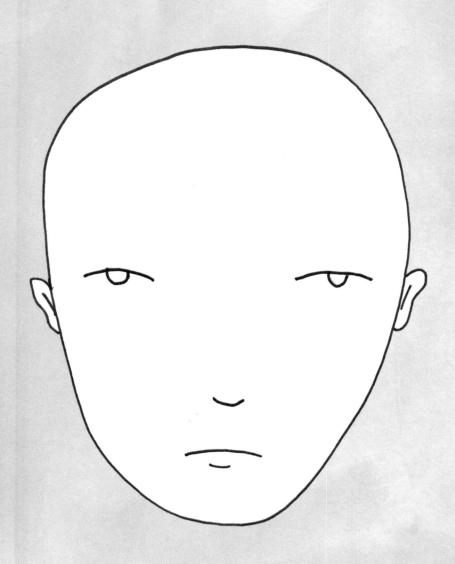

Draw your mom and dad the way you would have when you were six years old.

color in the squares to make a flower.

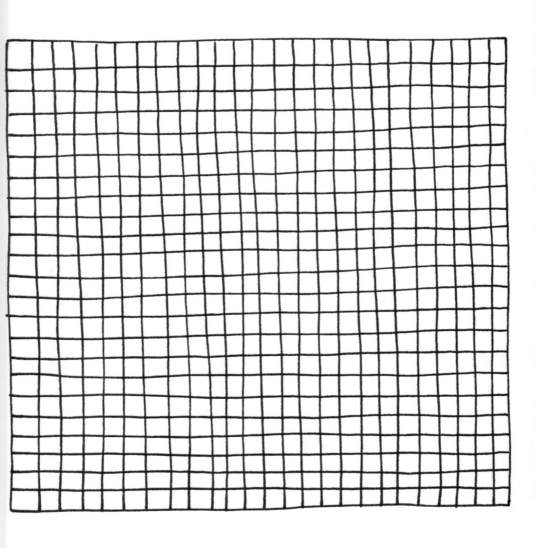

Here is a scribble:

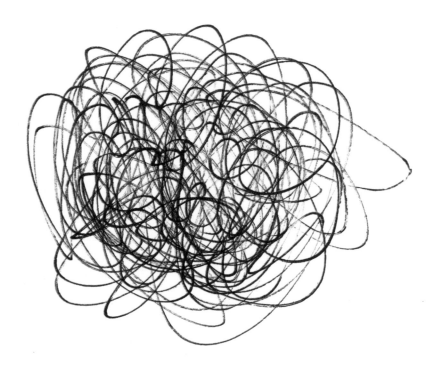

Scribbles are beautiful.
Each one is unique — you can't create
the same scribble twice.

And anybody can make one.

Your turn to make a beautiful scribble.

Add some color to it.

Design a tattoo for
someone who needs
a daily reminder
to be happy.

Draw something that rhymes with BOAT.

Make this person look OLD.

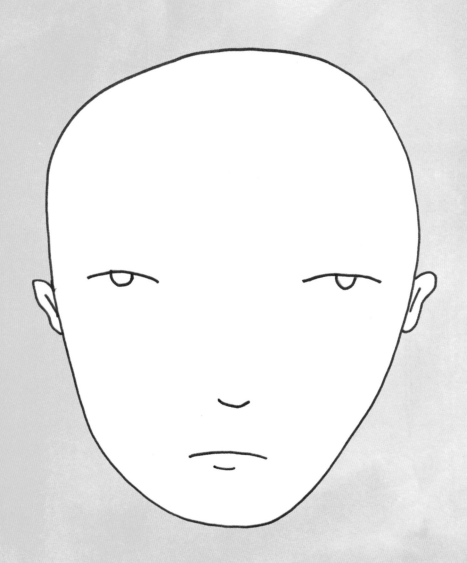

Connect the dots to make a GUITAR.

Draw some amazing pants.

What would you like to see right now?
Draw a reflection of it
in these glasses.

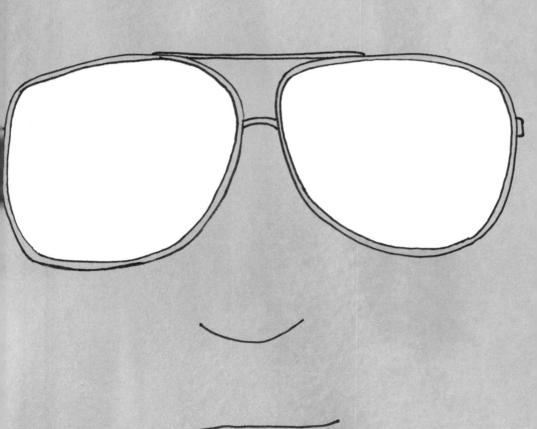

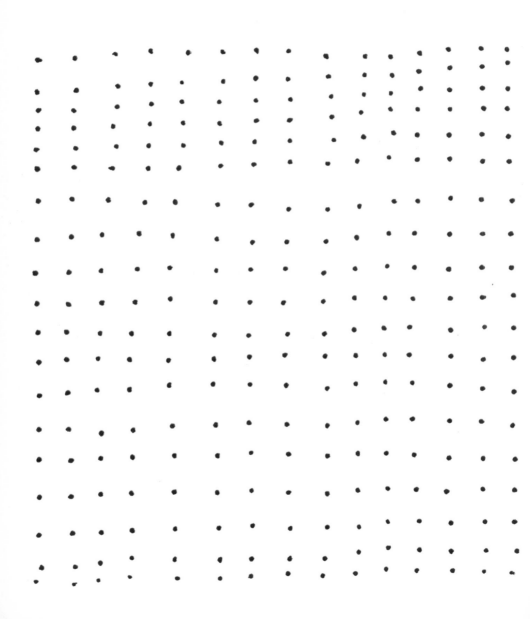

Design
a tattoo
for
someone
who
loves
books.

Draw a nice tree.

Now draw an upside down tree.
Don't turn the book around
until you've finished it!

Decorate this mug for someone who enjoys a calming cup of tea.

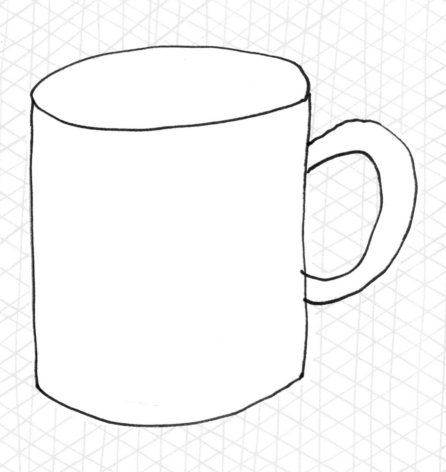

Make this woman look TIRED.

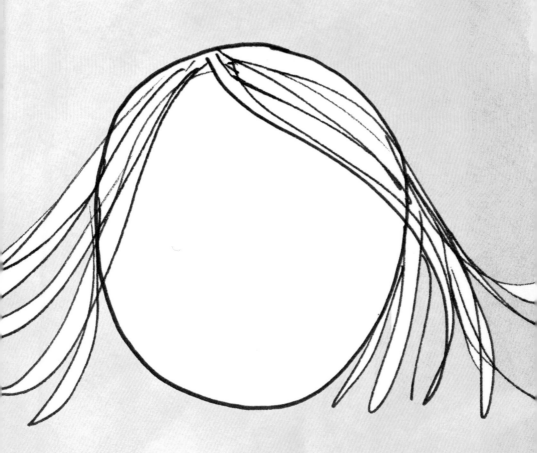

Connect the dots to make a FLAME.

Turn this into something.

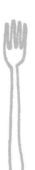

Draw your favorite meal.

Decorate this tote bag with a pattern (stripes, zig zags, dots, checkerboard, etc.).

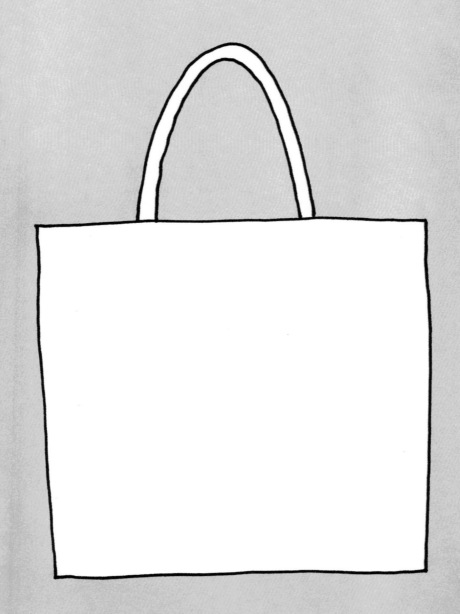

Draw your favorite tools
you use to create.

Using only triangles, draw a WATERING CAN.

Connect the dots to make a TURTLE.

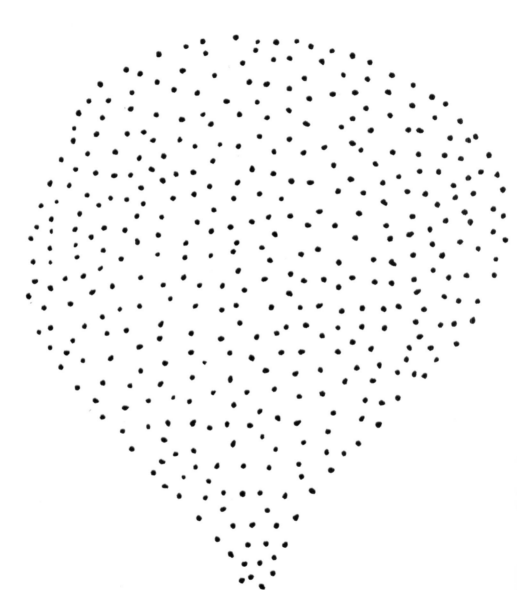

What's inside this house?
Draw what you see in the window.

Turn this into something.

Make this person look ANGRY.

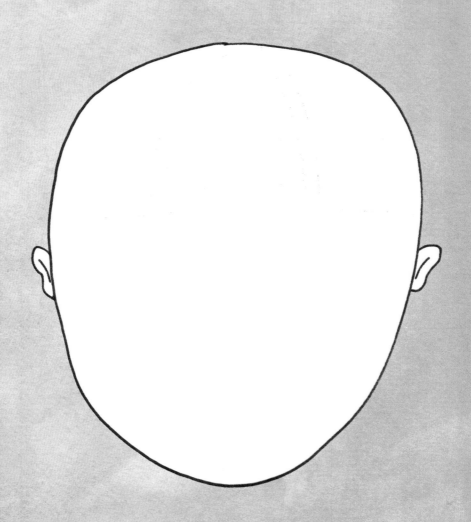

Decorate this tote bag with a face (or just an eye, or just lips...).

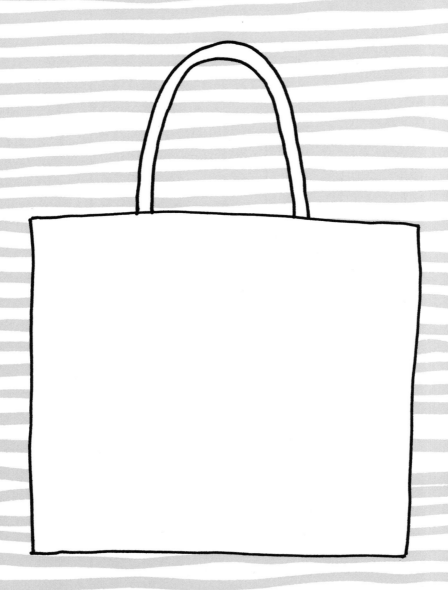

Draw all the ingredients of
your favorite recipe.

Turn this into something.

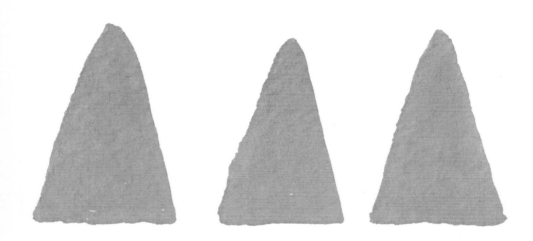

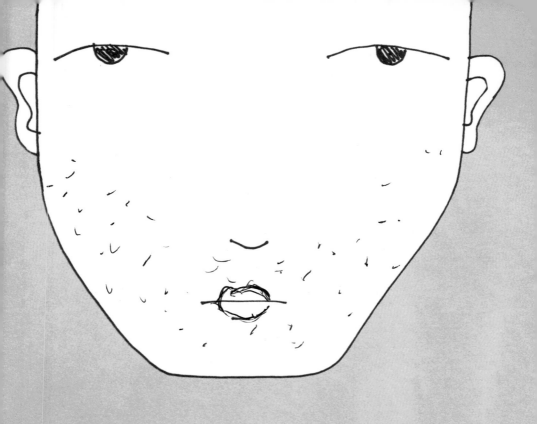

Draw a beard on this man.

(stubble? Goatee? Neatly clipped beard? You decide.)

Here is a grid:

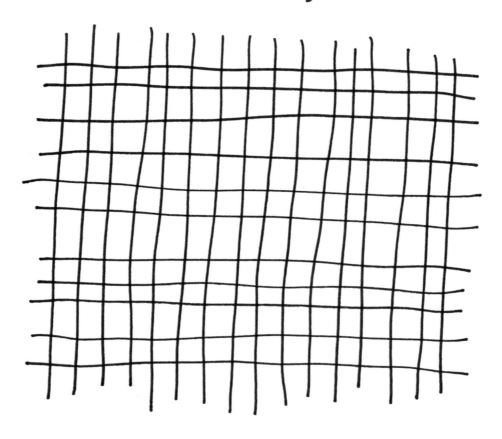

It's kind of loose, but that's okay.

There's a beautiful, pleasing, comfortable rhythm to a hand drawn grid.

Okay, your turn. Draw a grid.
(Don't try to copy mine.
Yours will be better.). I hate it.

Add some color.

(You could fill in random squares and
make a nice little abstract piece.)

Turn this into something. Anything!

Decorate these socks.

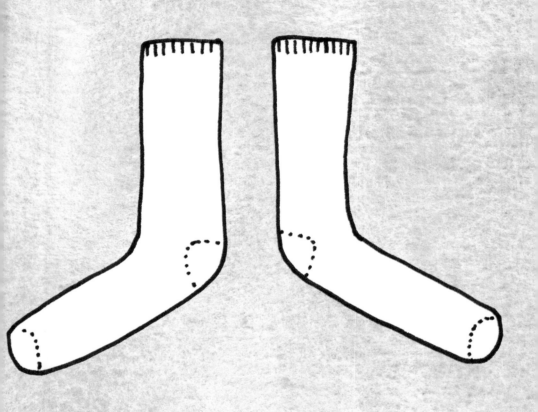

Using only triangles, draw a VOLCANO.

Make a line or a scribble
or an image that expresses
FRUSTRATION.

(Yup! That looks like frustration!)

Connect the dots to make a
PAIR OF GLASSES.

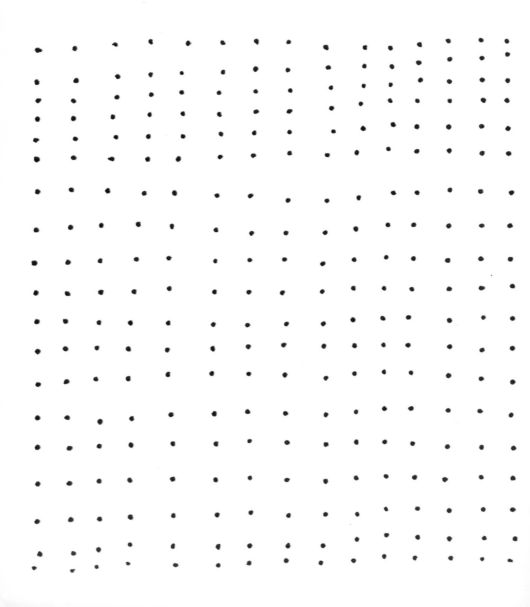

I'm no good at drawing horses.
Look: See? I told you.

what are you bad at drawing? Draw it here.

Design knuckle tattoos for someone who loves dogs.

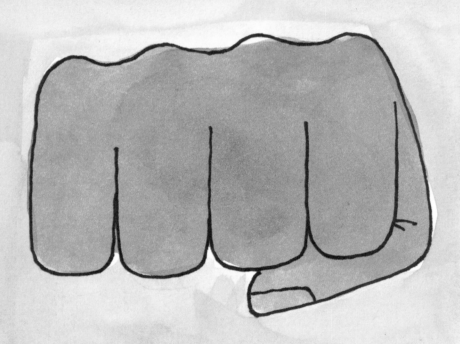

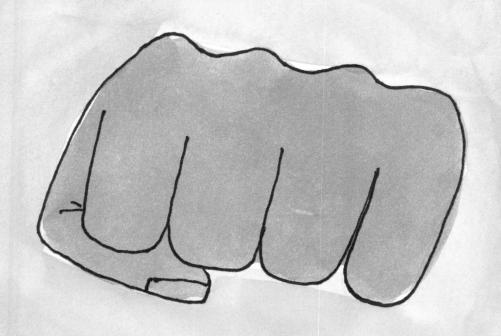

Make this man look TIRED.

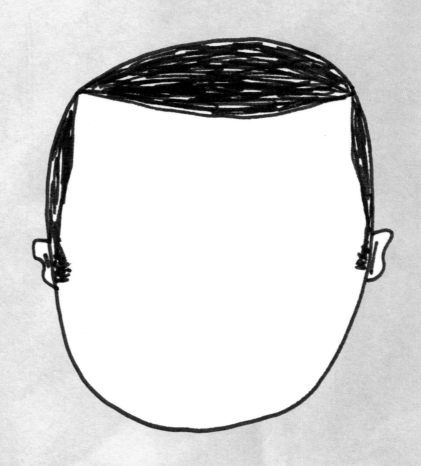

Draw something that rhymes with JACKET.

Using only triangles, draw a SHOE.

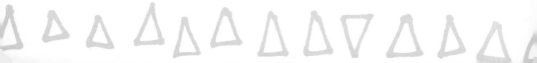

Turn this into something.

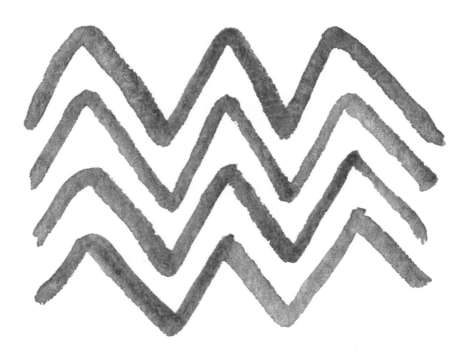

Make a line or a scribble
or an image that expresses
CALM.

(Aaaah. So nice.)

Turn this into something.

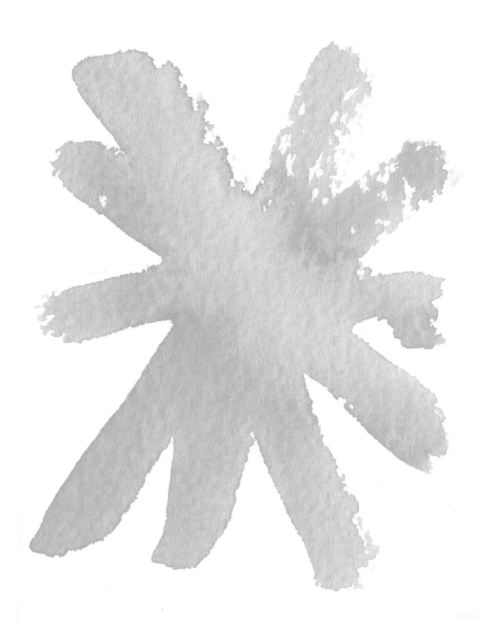

Draw ABSOLUTE JOY!